My First NFL Book

WASHINGTON REDSKINS

Steven M. Karras

www.av2books.com

LET'S READ

AV²
BY WEIGL™

ADDED VALUE • AUDIO VISUAL

Go to **www.av2books.com**, and enter this book's unique code.

BOOK CODE

N 5 6 7 2 8 7

AV² by Weigl brings you media enhanced books that support active learning.

AV² provides enriched content that supplements and complements this book. Weigl's AV² books strive to create inspired learning and engage young minds in a total learning experience.

Your AV² Media Enhanced books come alive with...

Audio
Listen to sections of the book read aloud.

Video
Watch informative video clips.

Embedded Weblinks
Gain additional information for research.

Try This!
Complete activities and hands-on experiments.

Key Words
Study vocabulary, and complete a matching word activity.

Quizzes
Test your knowledge.

Slide Show
View images and captions, and prepare a presentation.

... and much, much more!

Published by AV² by Weigl
350 5th Avenue, 59th Floor
New York, NY 10118

Website: www.av2books.com

Library of Congress Control Number: 2017930846

ISBN 978-1-4896-5568-4 (hardcover)
ISBN 978-1-4896-5570-7 (multi-user eBook)

Printed in the United States of America in Brainerd, Minnesota
1 2 3 4 5 6 7 8 9 0   21 20 19 18 17

032017
020317

Editor: Katie Gillespie
Art Director: Terry Paulhus

Weigl acknowledges Getty Images and iStock as the primary image suppliers for this title.

WASHINGTON REDSKINS

CONTENTS

Team History

The Washington Redskins joined the NFL in 1932. They were first called the Boston Braves. The name changed to the Redskins in their second year. The team moved to Washington, D.C., in 1937. The Redskins were the first team to have their entire season aired on TV.

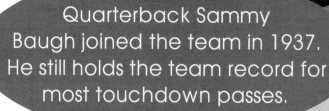

Quarterback Sammy Baugh joined the team in 1937. He still holds the team record for most touchdown passes.

5

The Stadium

FedExField has been the Redskins' home stadium since 1997. It was first called Jack Kent Cooke Stadium. Cooke was a former team owner. All of the seating levels are named after former Redskins players, coaches, or owners.

FedExField is in Landover, Maryland. This town is about 10 miles from Washington, D.C.

Team Spirit

The Redskins are one of only two NFL teams to have a marching band. The band plays "Hail to the Redskins." This is the team's fight song. The band performs before games and during halftime.

The Washington Redskins Marching Band formed on August 9, 1937.

The Jerseys

The Redskins' home jerseys are burgundy with white numbers. They are one of only three teams to have the players' numbers written on the sleeve instead of on the shoulder. "Redskins" is written below the collar.

The Helmet

The Redskins' helmet is burgundy. The team's logo is on each side. The logo is a Native American with two feathers in his hair. The idea for the logo came from a Native American named Walter "Blackie" Wetzel.

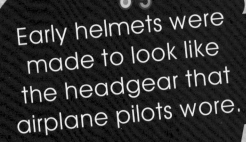

Early helmets were made to look like the headgear that airplane pilots wore.

13

14

The Coach

Jay Gruden is the Redskins' head coach. He was hired in 2014. Gruden played football before becoming a coach. He also coached the Cincinnati Bengals. Gruden led the Redskins to the playoffs in 2015. This was their first time in a playoff game since 2012.

Player Positions

A tight end is a position on the offense. Tight ends have two main jobs. One job is to block the defense. This lets other players on the offense get the ball. Their other job is to catch passes from the quarterback.

A fumble happens when a player loses control of the ball.

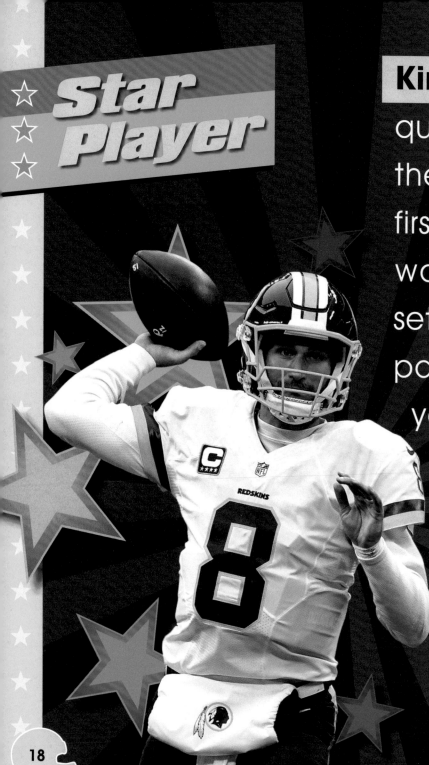

Kirk Cousins is a quarterback. He joined the Redskins in 2012. His first NFL touchdown pass was 77 yards. Cousins set a team record for passing the ball 4,166 yards in one season. He was one of only two NFL quarterbacks to throw a touchdown in all 16 regular season games.

Joe Theismann was a quarterback. He played with the Redskins for 12 seasons. Theismann was the team's quarterback in two Super Bowls. He made 2,044 completed passes. This is a team record. He has another team record for throwing the ball 25,206 total yards. Theismann threw 160 touchdowns in his career.

Team Records

The Redskins have won three Super Bowls. Kicker Mark Moseley scored 1,208 points for the team. This is a team record. Wide receiver Charley Taylor has a team record of 90 touchdowns scored. He is also in the Pro Football Hall of Fame.

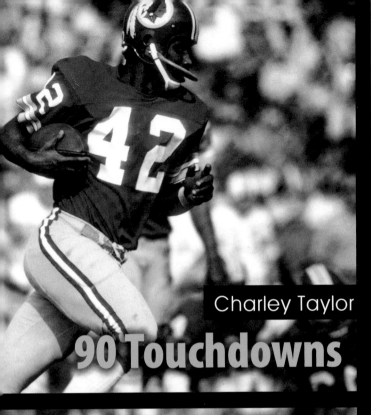

Charley Taylor

90 Touchdowns

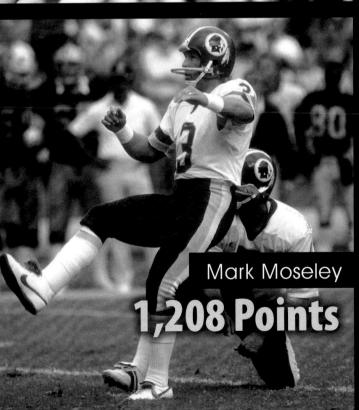

Mark Moseley

1,208 Points

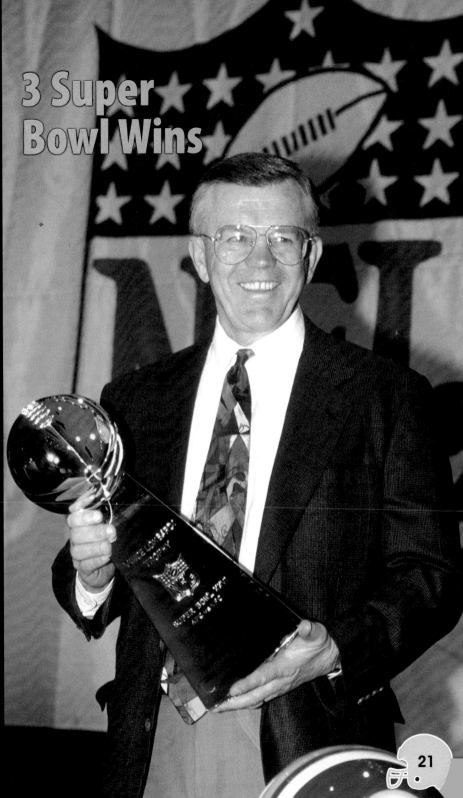

3 Super Bowl Wins

By the Numbers

The average number of people at a Redskins' home game is **81,064**.

The Redskins have **2** team chefs.

Cornerback Darrell Green set a team record for **295** games played.

25,000 people watched the Redskins' first home victory in Washington, D.C., in 1937.

The Redskins
once scored
72 points
in a single game. This
is an NFL record.

(21)

**Redskins players
are in the Pro
Football Hall
of Fame.**

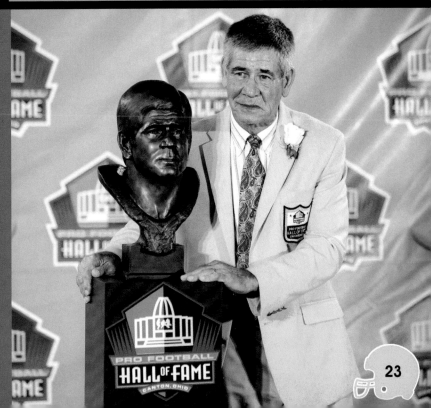

Quiz

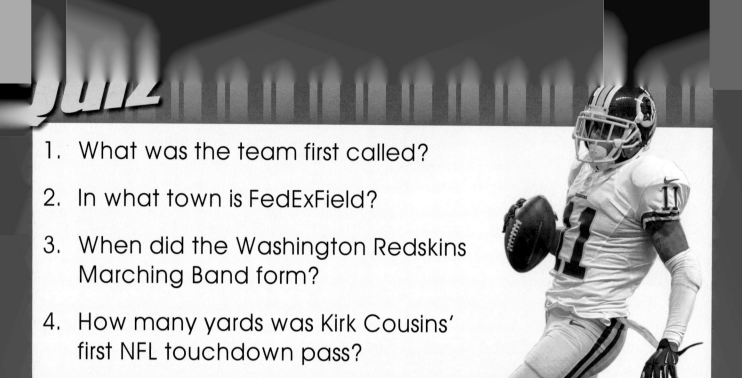

1. What was the team first called?

2. In what town is FedExField?

3. When did the Washington Redskins Marching Band form?

4. How many yards was Kirk Cousins' first NFL touchdown pass?

5. Who set a team record for 295 games played?

Check out www.av2books.com for activities, videos, audio clips, and more!

1 Go to www.av2books.com.

2 Enter book code. N 5 6 7 2 8 7

3 Fuel your imagination online!

www.av2books.com